COLONIAL PEOPLE

The Innkeeper

WIL MARA

 **Marshall Cavendish**
Benchmark
New York

This publication represents the opinions and views of the author based on Wil Mara's personal experience, knowledge, and research. The information in this book serves as a general guide only. The author and publisher have used their best efforts in preparing this book and disclaim liability rising directly and indirectly from the use and application of this book.

Other Marshall Cavendish Offices:
Marshall Cavendish International (Asia) Private Limited, 1 New Industrial Road, Singapore 536196 • Marshall Cavendish International (Thailand) Co. Ltd. 253 Asoke, 12th Flr, Sukhumvit 21 Road, Klongtoey Nua, Wattana, Bangkok 10110, Thailand • Marshall Cavendish (Malaysia) Sdn Bhd, Times Subang, Lot 46, Subang Hi-Tech Industrial Park, Batu Tiga, 40000 Shah Alam, Selangor Darul Ehsan, Malaysia

Marshall Cavendish is a trademark of Times Publishing Limited

All websites were available and accurate when this book was sent to press.

Library of Congress Cataloging-in-Publication Data

Mara, Wil.
The innkeeper / by Wil Mara. — 1st ed.
p. cm. — (Colonial people)
Includes bibliographical references and index.
Summary: "Explore the life of a colonial innkeeper and his importance to the community, as well as everyday life, responsibilities, and social practices during that time"—Provided by publisher.
ISBN 978-0-7614-4796-2
1. Hotelkeepers—United States—History—17th century—Juvenile literature. 2. United States—History—Colonial period, ca. 1600–1775—Juvenile literature. I. Title.
TX909.M317 2010
647.94092—dc22
2009011873

Editor: Christine Florie
Publisher: Michelle Bisson
Art Director: Anahid Hamparian
Series Designer: Kay Petronio

Expert Reader: Professor Paul Douglas Newman, Ph.D., Department of History, University of Pittsburgh at Johnstown

Photo research by Marybeth Kavanagh

Cover photo by Percy Moran/Library of Congress

The photographs in this book are used by permission and through the courtesy of:

The Image Works: 13; ARPL/HIP, 4; *Getty Images*: MPI, 7, 37; Hulton Archive, 33; *The Granger Collection*: 8, 25; *The Colonial Williamsburg Foundation*: 11, 14, 16, 23, 39; *Alamy*: North Wind Picture Archives, 19; *Old Sturbridge Village*, Sturbridge, MA: 22; *North Wind Picture Archives*: 30; *Photo Researchers, Inc.*: Andy Levin, 35

Printed in Malaysia (T)
1 3 5 6 4 2

CONTENTS

ONE

America's Colonial Period

In the mid– to late–1500s, thousands of people in Europe began taking ships across the Atlantic Ocean to come to North America. It was a long and sometimes dangerous journey, but this exciting new place seemed to have everything, including fresh farmland, unspoiled lakes and rivers, plentiful sources of food, miles of unexplored territory, and, perhaps best of all, greater personal freedom. These settlers came from many different European countries; and due to this interesting mix of races and customs, the United States—long before it was called that—became a great cultural "salad bowl." These brave travelers were known as colonists. A colony is a group of people who live separately from their homeland but are still under the rule of that land.

In 1620 Pilgrims sailed from England on their voyage to the New World.

The End of the Colonial Era

By the mid–1770s colonists were losing patience with the leaders of their European homelands. By this time, most were ruled by Great Britain. Britain was taking more and more money away from the colonists through a process called **taxation.** The angry colonists, however, often refused to pay. They began writing their own rules and laws, and they were also creating their own government—each colony sent a small group of people to Philadelphia, Pennsylvania, in 1774 to form the **First Continental Congress.** Then, on July 4, 1776, Congress adopted the Declaration of Independence—and the United States of America was born. This marked the end of Great Britain's rule—and the close of the colonial era in American history.

By the late 1600s and early 1700s, towns were being established with shops for blacksmithing, furniture making, and cloth weaving. North American wood was excellent for the construction of ships, so a shipbuilding industry arose. Soon, every large town along the eastern coast of North America had sailors coming and going each day. The fishing business also grew during the colonial era.

Colonists grew their own food, and many kept goats and cows for milk. Water was carried in buckets from a natural water source such as a stream or river. If there wasn't one nearby, a colonist had to dig a well. This sometimes meant digging down 30 or 40 feet. Water was also used to wash everyday items such as clothes, tablecloths, and bedsheets. The water was boiled in a large **cauldron**, heated by a small fire underneath. Once the items were clean, they were hung outside to dry. And the soap had to be made from scratch,

Colonial families usually grew their own food.

often using lye and animal fat. Soap was also used to clean a person's body and hair, but there were no showers. A colonist often had one bucket of clean water for this purpose, which was poured over the head after soaping up was finished. Brushing teeth involved rubbing each one with a fine cloth that was first dipped in water with a little salt added.

People got from place to place by walking, riding on horseback, or traveling in a horse-pulled cart, wagon, or carriage. Light came

In the colonies, many people traveled by walking or by horseback.

from candles or from lamps that burned oil. For fun, colonists played simple games such as marbles, read books, or enjoyed the company and conversation of friends and family. If someone did not have the money to buy something needed, it was not uncommon to trade for it. This is called bartering. A farmer with extra vegetables, for example, might give them to a wheelwright who fixed a broken wheel on one of the farmer's wagons.

Innkeepers were very important in colonial times. They provided food and shelter for travelers. Without the innkeeper to take in these weary strangers, America's growth would have taken even longer. The innkeeper also provided a place for people to sit and talk with one another, trade stories and ideas, and form friendships. Everyone's role in a colonial town made a difference, and people worked together to make one another's lives better. By knowing what innkeepers did, a lot can be learned about the early days of a great nation.

TWO

A Day in the Life of a Colonial Innkeeper

A colonial innkeeper, often called the **landlord**, needed to get up very early each morning. Once awake, he had to get right to work. Sometimes he would sleep in a clean set of clothes to avoid wasting time bathing in the morning. A splash of cool water on his face from a large washbasin was often enough. If the innkeeper had a staff, he would wake them next. Most colonial inns had at least one other worker apart from the owner. The staff might include hired laborers, **indentured servants**, slaves, or even family members. It was not at all unusual for an entire family to take part in the upkeep of an inn.

Mornings

Everyone had their own set of chores to perform each morning. The innkeeper would go to the backyard and gather wood for fires. He

The innkeeper's family had many daily chores. One was to pick fresh vegetables from their garden.

might also need to chop large logs into smaller pieces. Fires would be lit in the fireplaces in the kitchen for cooking and in the dining room or sitting room for warmth. Creating a cozy and inviting atmosphere for the guests on cold mornings was particularly important.

While the landlord was tending to the fires, the rest of the family would prepare the morning meal. If there was a garden out back, they would pick fresh fruits and vegetables. If they had farm animals, they would milk the cows and collect eggs from the chickens. Some even made their own butter and baked their own bread.

Corn, Corn, Everywhere

Corn was a common food item in colonial times. American Indians taught early settlers how to grow, harvest, and store it. Dried corn kernels would often have to be crushed into fine bits with the help of a **mortar and pestle** or a grinding wheel. This was often done by a miller, who would then sell the ground cornmeal at a local market. Cornmeal was an important ingredient in making bread, pudding, pie, porridge, and many other foods. Corn kernels could also be used to feed chickens, and corn stalks were eaten by cattle. Corn husks were used for everything from mattress stuffing to toys and decorations. Cobs could also be used as animal feed, plus as the bowls for pipes and the stoppers for jugs.

Guests would begin coming down for breakfast at various times; some might have asked the innkeeper to wake them at a particular hour. The dining room often featured one large table, maybe two; and everyone would eat together. Sometimes travelers' faces were familiar to the innkeeper and the staff—people who had become regulars through their frequent stays during business trips. Others were strangers from distant lands, and they would entertain their fellow visitors with stories of the faraway places from which they came. The innkeeper always made sure the breakfast table was neatly set.

Typical breakfast foods included grits, corn mush, porridge, cooked eggs, waffles, and pancakes (often called flapjacks or johnnycakes). Ham would be served either boiled or cold; and bacon was offered in many places, along with a variety of fish and salted meats. Bread and cheese were also available, as was fresh milk, plus a selection of juices, ciders, coffee, and tea. Every table also had containers of salt, pepper, sugar, butter, cream,

At breakfast, guests at an inn would share the same table.

and syrup. Many guests liked to cover their biscuits with gravy, grease, or lard. Whatever choices a guest made, it was the staff's duty to make sure every customer left the table with a full stomach. A traveler from England who stayed in a New York inn wrote, "They breakfast at eight o'clock upon rump steaks, fish, eggs, and a variety of cakes with tea or coffee."

After breakfast the dining tables would be cleared off and scrubbed clean. The dishes and cups or mugs were taken away and washed with boiling water, often in huge cauldrons hung over small fires. If a guest was leaving, the innkeeper would present the person with a bill for services—the cost of the night's stay plus whatever food and drink were consumed. Prices were kept low, often by law; however, innkeepers still made a profit. If a guest needed directions, the innkeeper would write them down or draw a map. In larger towns, inns could become very busy during the day. During quiet moments between meals, the innkeeper might

An innkeeper kept track of his daily expenses by recording how much he spent and earned.

also tend to the books, in which were kept records of who came and went, how much they were charged, and so on. An innkeeper had to keep track of how much money was spent compared to how much was made.

If an inn did not have its own garden, the staff would visit local farms or other markets to get fresh food. Fruits and vegetables would be collected, as well as spices and salted meats. Sometimes an inn was also used as a **meetinghouse**, similar to today's houses of worship, where townspeople would gather and hold a religious service. When this happened, the innkeeper would have to rearrange the furniture in one of the larger rooms in order to accommodate the worshipers.

Afternoons

Lunch, like breakfast, was a bountiful affair. A variety of meats were common, as animals were abundant and hunting them was a normal part of colonial life. Wild birds such as quail, pheasants, and partridges were frequent menu items, as were domesticated birds such as chickens. Deer and bear meat were also available as long as those animals were found locally, as well as farm-raised lamb and beef. Different types of soups and stews provided a healthy and filling meal for a reasonable price.

After lunch the innkeeper's staff would tend to the bedrooms, sweeping the floors and changing the sheets. The bedding had to be boiled, wrung out, and then hung on a line in the yard. If it was too cold outside, they would be hung indoors. Not all inns offered sheets to their guests. Some had only common beds made mostly of straw, and guests were expected to sleep in their clothes or on blankets they brought themselves. Guests might be able to get their dirty clothes washed by the inn staff but would be charged a fee for the service.

For an extra fee, guests could have their clothes washed by the inn's staff.

The innkeeper would tend to repairs around the inn during the afternoon hours. He might also be responsible for sorting and delivering mail; in many colonial towns and villages, there were no post offices. Thus, travelers might arrive with packages or letters that they would leave in the care of a local innkeeper. Sometimes an innkeeper also had a second job, such as that of a blacksmith, politician, or **deacon**, and would tend to those duties while the inn was relatively quiet.

Evenings

Dinner would be served in the late afternoon or early evening. The typical inn served a basic meal of beer or **hard cider**, plus a warm stew with bread. Some of the finer inns, however, had a greater selection. For the main course, these places offered everything from boiled chicken, pork, mutton, and tongue to mince pies, oyster patties, and a variety of fish. Common vegetables included tomatoes, squash, cauliflower, beets, onions, spinach, eggplant, and a selection of potatoes. Other popular side dishes were rice, beans, raisins, and several different kinds of nuts. Homemade pudding and custard were standard desserts.

After dinner the innkeeper had to make sure his guests were sufficiently entertained. Sometimes a local musician would come

Making a Colonial Stew

Most inns served a warm, hearty stew for dinner. If you would like to try to make your own colonial stew, follow these simple directions with the help of an adult.

Things You Will Need

2 tablespoons butter

1 pound lean beef, cut into
   1-inch pieces

8 tomatoes

5 carrots, peeled

3 celery stalks

2 potatoes, peeled

1 onion, peeled (optional)

1 cup of peas

1 cup of cut green beans

1 cup of corn

salt and pepper

1 tablespoon minced garlic

5 cups water

Directions

1. Preheat a large pan or skillet, and add butter. When the butter has melted, add the meat and let it brown on medium-high heat.

2. Wash and then cut the whole vegetables into small pieces. Put the vegetables in a soup pot. Combine with 1 teaspoon each of salt and pepper, the minced garlic, and the water.

3. Set the soup pot on a burner and bring the water to a boil.

4. Add the beef and stir, then reduce heat to low and let the stew simmer for one hour, or until the beef is fully cooked. Remember to stir the pot occasionally so the contents will not stick to the bottom of the pot.

Evenings at an inn were a time for townspeople and guests to meet and talk about current events.

and sing or play an instrument. Simple games such as checkers and marbles were popular. But perhaps the most common form of nightly entertainment was simple conversation. Local townspeople would visit a busy inn to chat not only with the owner and the workers but also with the many visitors who were passing through. Sitting in a warm, firelit room with friends was a great source of pleasure in colonial times.

By nine or ten o'clock guests would begin to head up to their rooms. It was common in colonial times for a guest to share a room with another guest, who was usually a complete stranger. Meanwhile, the innkeeper and the workers would do the last of the cleaning up, put out any remaining fires, and turn down the oil lamps. In some towns, it was required that all lights be put out before the innkeeper went to sleep—a light burning in the middle of the night was often considered a sign of trouble. Sometimes a new guest would arrive late from a long journey, in which case the innkeeper was obligated to give the traveler a room regardless of the hour.

THREE

A Colonial Inn

Most colonial inns looked like ordinary homes rather than formal hotels. In fact, many were exactly that—large homes with enough extra rooms to be used as resting places for travelers. Thus, inns varied greatly in size, shape, general construction, and so on. Some were large and stately, whereas others appeared to be little more than rundown roadhouses. If a traveler needed to stop somewhere to sleep for the night, the choices could be very limited.

On the Outside

One item common to inns was a **signboard** out front, either attached to the wall (often near the door) or hanging from a rod or a post. It was usually made of wood, stone, or metal, and either carved or painted (or both). Innkeepers wanted their signs to be as simple as possible but also unique enough to catch the attention of all who passed by. The signmaker would come up with an image that was somehow associated with the inn. There might be a bed or

This inn's sign features a patriotic theme with an American eagle carrying a shield and arrows.

a mug or a plate with a fork and knife on either side. Sometimes the designs were patriotic, with an eagle or a flag. Other signboards were humorous, with an animal smiling or wearing glasses.

Colonial inns also needed to have at least one **hitching post** in front. A hitching post was in fact made up of three posts—two posts sticking out of the ground and a longer post set on top of them. The hitching post gave visitors a place to tie up their horses so the animals wouldn't wander off. After a horse was secured, one of the inn workers might come out to supply food and water, and maybe even give the animal a good brushing. If the inn had a stable or corral in back, the horse would be kept there as long as the guest stayed. That way it would be safe from horse thieves or predatory animals.

The property surrounding a colonial inn had many interesting features, all dedicated to the welfare and comfort of the inn's customers. There might be a large garden or even a few acres of farmland, where fresh fruits and vegetables would be grown. There would also be commonplace livestock such as cows, goats, chickens, and roosters. In the colonial era, farmland could provide not only for the inn's guests, but also for the owner and his family.

Many colonial inns featured a garden or farm that included livestock.

One colonial innkeeper wrote, "Nothing to eat, drink, or wear was bought, as my farm provided all."

Large cauldrons or washbasins set outside would be used to clean sheets, tablecloths, napkins, and clothing. Water was drawn either from a well or through an underground pump. It was not unusual to see fallen trees waiting to be chopped for firewood or wood already cut and stacked in neat piles. In warmer weather inn workers would make their own beer, wine, or hard cider. Butter was made in large wooden **churns**. At many inns, even candles were made by hand; animal fat or whale oil would be boiled and then poured into wooden molds. Candle making was very common in colonial days, as was the making of soap.

On the Inside

The inside of a colonial inn was usually sparse and simple. Most inns had a sitting room, similar to the modern living room in terms of purpose. The floorboards were often bare, dusty, and creaky. Sometimes they would be covered by a large rug or two. There might be a couch, but more often than not there were a collection of wooden chairs and tables, and timbered beams ran across the ceiling. A sitting room might also feature a small bar where everything from beer and wine to rum and cider was

The kitchen of a colonial inn was a busy room bustling with staff preparing the daily meals.

served. A sitting room with a bar would then be known as a barroom, or a **taproom**.

The inn kitchen was always abuzz with activity. One of the most remarkable features was the hearth, which was very large and often had several fires going at once. The opening could be 5 or 6 feet high and as much as 7 or 8 feet wide—enough space for several people to stand in. The actual purpose was, of course, to allow plenty of room for cooking. Soups and stew pots were hung from iron hooks, and meat was roasted over an open flame after being stuck on a spit—a short pole with a handle for cranking on one end—so the meat could be turned slowly and cooked evenly. Pans had long handles so the cooks wouldn't burn themselves while frying fish or slices of pork and chicken. Toasting forks, also with long handles, were ideal for cooking small items individually, and kettles provided boiling water for tea.

Next to the fireplace was a smaller opening known as the stone oven. It was used primarily for baking, mostly bread. It would be stuffed with small pieces of wood, which were then set ablaze until a bed of steadily burning embers was produced. Once it was warm enough inside, freshly formed bread loaves were slid inside on a flat piece of wood called a peel and then left to bake slowly and thoroughly on the hot stone surface.

Bedrooms often had individual names, such as the Sun Room or East Room or Red Room. This not only made it easy for the innkeeper and the staff to identify each room; it also gave the inn a certain amount of charm and character. An inn bedroom was, like the rest of the establishment, usually very simple in terms of decoration and furnishings. A typical bed would be nothing more than a simple bag of straw, and the floor on which it sat might not even be covered with wood—if it was on the first floor, it could be

The Best of the Best

A few colonial inns developed a reputation for supplying the greatest comfort and pleasure to their guests. These became known throughout the colonies, and many people would stop there just for the experience. For a little more money, they could have meals cooked exactly as they wished (instead of having to choose from a menu). Windows might have wool or linen curtains, the pillows and mattresses were usually stuffed with various feathers, and the bed was often the four-poster variety, which was very popular in colonial times. Most inn bedrooms had a few chairs or benches, a dresser, and a table with a small washbasin. Candles or oil lamps were also available. Some inns might also furnish a writing desk and a small fireplace. A visitor's horses would be fed, watered, and given a good brushing—and on a cold night they would be kept in a private stall and covered with a blanket.

the very dirt upon which the house sat. Windows usually did not have glass but rather a pair of wooden shutters.

The People

Perhaps the most important feature of any colonial inn was the people who ran it. It is interesting to note that many innkeepers were women. The colonial period was, for the most part, a male-dominated era, so it was unusual for a woman to hold a position of ownership. This was partly because a large percentage of women in those days were widows. The colonial period was often brutally hard on men, many of whom either died from overwork, accidents, or battles with American Indians. Many colonial women turned out to be superb innkeepers.

The staff could consist of people from all walks of life. Family-owned inns usually enlisted the efforts of everyone from the husband and wife to the youngest children. It was not unusual to see a young boy chopping wood in the backyard while his little sister cut vegetables with her mother in the kitchen. Successful inns were often passed down from one generation to the next, with the children having the advantage of already knowing how to manage the business by a very early age. Other workers might be local laborers hired on a per-hour basis or black slaves who were already owned by the innkeeper.

FOUR

The Inn and the Colonial Community

The inn held a place of high regard and importance in the average colonial community. It was seen, for example, as not just a place where travelers could rest for a night or two and get food and water for their horses, but also as a social hot spot, where town gossip was exchanged along with new ideas and observations.

A Gathering Place

If a person walked into a sitting room or taproom and found a big crowd, there was a good chance the majority of those in attendance were not guests of the inn, but rather leading local figures discussing important issues. Thus, an inn could also act as a kind of political battleground. Future U.S. president John Adams, upon visiting an establishment in Shrewsbury, Massachusetts, wrote,

Colonial inns were a good place to meet people of local importance and make friends.

"There presently came in, one after another, half a dozen, or half a score substantial yeoman of the neighborhood, who, sitting down to the fire after lighting their pipes, began a lively conversation on politics."

Making Plans, Taking Action

Inns and taverns not only served as places where people could talk about politics, but also where they could take action against unfair political practices. In the mid–1700s, when the colonists' anger toward the government of Great Britain began to reach its height, inns and taverns were often used as headquarters for groups of people who wanted to break free of Great Britain's control. These people were known as Patriots, whereas those who wanted to stay loyal to Great Britain were called Loyalists. Inns and taverns throughout the colonies often provided Patriots with safe places to meet and plan their activities on the road to America's independence.

Goodwill

Almost every colonial town had at least one inn. In the colonial era, it was considered a sign of low morals for a town to disregard the needs of weary travelers. Many counties, in fact, required this by law; towns that did not obey were frequently given large fines. One innkeeper in Massachusetts wrote, "For want of an ordinary, [the town was] twice fined by the county, and would have been a third time had I not undertaken it." (An ordinary was another name for an inn.) People who owned houses ideally suited for inn business were sometimes offered attractive rewards (called incentives) to become landlords, even if only on a part-time basis. They might be given extra land on which to expand their crops or allow their animals to graze and roam. They might have had their taxes lowered or improvements made to their property at the town's expense.

Another town policy concerning inns was the discouragement of high prices. In other words, innkeepers were not allowed to overcharge their guests. Although exact prices were not usually dictated to innkeepers, they were supposed to be kept relatively low and reasonable. If a traveler or family of very little means arrived, most innkeepers would feed them and let them stay for free. In the southern colonies, where inns were often part of vast plantation estates, guests were routinely allowed to stay without cost. Most would still, just as a matter of honor, give the innkeeper some small payment to show their appreciation (and help cover the expenses).

Another vital community function of the colonial inn was to support soldiers during times of war. If any battles occurred nearby or if soldiers were simply passing through, innkeepers were morally bound to provide them with food and lodging. While the soldiers were there, local women would often bring them food in appreciation of their service. If a battle did occur close by, an inn might also end up being transformed into a makeshift hospital, temporarily caring for the wounded until they could be moved to more appropriate quarters.

Regardless of all this goodwill, most innkeepers still turned a respectable profit for themselves. Running an inn was particularly lucrative in the busier cities, where thousands came every week to conduct business or stop during a longer journey elsewhere. Perhaps the best money was made by the inns that were located near seaports, which were always very busy and brought interesting people from all over the world. Sea travel was common in colonial times, and innkeepers could count on a great amount of business if they had a steady stream of sailors arriving on their doorstep.

The Religious Influence

Inns were often considered as important to a colonial community as their churches and meetinghouses. This was especially true in the New

The most profitable inns were located near seaports because so many people came and went every day.

England colonies, which were heavily populated by Puritans—a group of people who took their devotion to God very seriously in every aspect of their lives. Houses of worship, therefore, were at the very heart of these colonial towns and cities. During religious days, innkeepers were often required to essentially chase out all of their guests—even if they were strangers from other places just passing through—so they would have time to attend services.

Whereas the northern colonies had a great religious influence that reached into the daily operation of their inns, such rules were a little softer in the South. There, communities had more open space—for example, it was not unusual for one person to own 50 acres of land and for houses to be anywhere from a few hundred yards to a half mile or more apart from one another. Thus, many southern innkeepers were free to observe—or ignore—whatever rules they saw fit. For instance, the use of tobacco (for smoking or chewing, or as **snuff**) was prohibited in many northern colonies. In the South, however, people could use tobacco freely.

A Person of Character

People who owned and managed inns were usually those of fair to high importance in colonial communities. They had to be individuals of good standing, with solid reputations for steadiness and reliability. They also had to have hospitable and cheerful natures, because inns run by dour, unpleasant sorts didn't remain open for long. One traveler at the time noted, "To provide safety for and comfort against danger and mischief [town leaders] took particular pains in their laws to prevent inns from being kept by unprincipled or worthless men."

Innkeepers were also considered a kind of town representative, because they were the people in their communities who had the most contact with visitors from other places. Travelers who had sailed from England or France, for example, might build their entire impression of a town upon their interactions with an innkeeper or the service they received.

Innkeepers were highly regarded members of the colonial community.

FIVE

Inns and the Law

In colonial times, law enforcement officials had tremendous power and influence over their communities. They could walk into people's homes at will and arrest someone at a moment's notice, even if they only suspected a person of committing a crime. A crime was often defined as whatever a town's leaders said it was, and there were times when it seemed as if they were inventing the rules as they went along.

Leaders and Spies

Mayors and law enforcement officials were not the only ones who decided what was right or wrong in a colonial community; religious leaders were deeply respected and even feared in this regard. A colonial town's religious leader would make frequent visits to the local inn just to make sure everyone was behaving. If he witnessed any activity of which he disapproved, he would either order it stopped or chase out the people involved.

A Puritan minister scolds his fellow settlers outside the town's inn.

Inns were good places to find lawbreakers and evildoers, largely because so many people came and went from other towns. Many innkeepers were required to participate in these spying activities. Even if they didn't wish to, they were compelled by the threat of punishment. A stranger from a distant place might be welcomed with a hearty handshake and a warm hello from an innkeeper, but he would also be studied closely for the duration of his stay. Particularly in the **puritanical** New England colonies, guests were expected to forget about the ways of their hometown and obey the rules of the town they were visiting. If, for example, a southerner stopped in Massachusetts for a night and was caught sitting outside smoking tobacco through a pipe—which might be perfectly acceptable in his home state of, say, North Carolina—he might receive a fine. The innkeeper would also be fined for not reporting the incident.

Innkeepers were sometimes given lists of local people who were considered criminals, and they were not allowed to provide them with food or housing under any circumstances. If anyone on the list arrived at the inn, the innkeeper was expected either to arrest and detain the individual himself or, at the very least, alert local authorities. There was some sense in this—every now and then a truly dangerous person who was on the run might seek shelter on a cold or rainy night, in which case an innkeeper had the opportunity to help capture him.

The Evils of Drink

Laws and views on the drinking of alcohol in a colonial inn varied greatly from town to town. Even in the New England colonies it was tolerated to a certain degree. As long as a person behaved, most towns did not seem to mind how much one drank. The main reason for this, most likely, is the fact that a town made so much money through the sale of beer, wine, and hard liquor. They did this through the collection of a **tithe**—a tax on the money brought in by innkeepers through their taprooms. The men who collected tithes were known as **tithing men**, and they were often the same people who walked around making sure law and order were always being maintained. The sale of alcohol became a cash bonanza for a colonial town—money was made if you drank just a little, and money was made if you drank too much.

The drinking of alcohol in colonial inns was allowed, though the laws varied from town to town.

When someone was punished for public drunkenness, he might serve a night in jail or pay a fine. Sometimes he was locked in the **stocks**—a set of framed wooden planks with holes for holding the feet and the hands (and sometimes the head). Stocks were usually set in the middle of a town so people walking by would see who was being punished. While a few hours in the stocks were certainly painful to one's body, the humiliation was often much worse.

Merriment and Other Crimes

Along with drinking, other forms of merriment were frowned upon in the more puritanical areas. Dancing was allowed in some places, but many forbade it. Gambling was also discouraged—simply carrying a pack of cards or a set of dice could get you in trouble. So did using foul language. In some of the most puritanical villages, whistling, laughing too loudly, or even speaking to a married woman were all grounds for punishment. One record from Boston shows that a man was fined for cursing, another for throwing a **beer-pot**, and a third for lying. The challenge for the average innkeeper in this type of community was to satisfy customers and local leaders at the same time.

Landlord, law officer, laborer, bartender, postal worker, spy . . . the innkeeper had to be all of these things and more. In many ways, that person was the eyes and ears of a colonial community, knowing every name, overhearing conversations, greeting hungry strangers, and trying to make an honest living through it all. An innkeeper could be young, old, male, female; it didn't matter. But the individual could not be lazy, for there was too much to do each day. Being an innkeeper in colonial times was one of the most challenging of all professions, one that played a key role in the formation of the United States during the nation's slow march to independence.

Glossary

beer-pot   a large open container for holding beer

cauldron   a large iron pot set over a fire for cooking or cleaning

churn   a tall, cylindrical wooden container with a long stick protruding from the top, used to make butter

deacon   second in rank under a priest or pastor and often considered his assistant

First Continental Congress   men who gathered to represent the people of twelve of the thirteen colonies in 1774, in Philadelphia

hard cider   a powerful drink made from the fermented juice of crushed apples

hitching post   a structure consisting of a horizontal wooden beam set upon two smaller vertical beams, to which horses could be tied

indentured servant   a person who agrees to work for another for a set period of time, after which that individual is given his or her freedom

landlord   the head of an inn, usually the owner

meetinghouse   a place where townspeople would engage in religious worship

mortar and pestle   tools used to crush and grind

puritanical   very strict in moral and religious matters

signboard	a sign in front of an inn used to attract customers, usually carved and/or colorfully painted
snuff	powdered tobacco inhaled through the nose
stocks	a set of framed wooden planks with holes for holding the feet, the hands, and sometimes the head, used as punishment for minor crimes in some colonial towns
taproom	similar to a sitting room, except with a bar for the serving of alcoholic beverages
taxation	the act of paying a small portion of one's income to a government
tithe	similar to a tax
tithing men	in colonial times, the men charged with the duty of collecting tithes/taxes

Find Out More

BOOKS

Johnson, Terry, compiler. *What Really Happened in Colonial Times*. Mississauga, ON: Knowledge Quest Books, 2007.

Kalman, Bobby. *A Visual Dictionary of a Colonial Community*. New York: Crabtree Publishing, 2008.

Prescott, Della. *A Day in a Colonial Home*. Carlisle, MA: Applewood Books, 2006.

Roberts, Russell. *Life in Colonial America*. Hockessin, DE: Mitchell Lane Publishers, 2007.

Stille, Darlene R. *Anne Hutchinson, Puritan Protester*. Mankato, MN: Compass Point Books, 2006.

DVD

Liberty's Kids. Shout! Factory, 2008.

WEBSITES

Colonial Williamsburg

www.history.org/almanack/life/trades/tradehdr.cfm

This site features a list of common tradespeople in colonial Williamsburg, Virginia.

Kid Info

www.kidinfo.com/American_History/Colonization_Colonial_Life.html

This website features many excellent links and loads of useful information on the thirteen colonies, colonial clothing, food, and government, just to name a few.

Social Studies for Kids
www.socialstudiesforkids.com/subjects/colonialtimes.htm

Social Studies for Kids has many excellent links on the life and times in colonial America.

Index

About the Author

Wil Mara has written more than a hundred books, many of which are educational titles for young readers. A full bibliography of his work can be found at www.wilmara.com.